WITHDRAWN

MOUNTAIN TOWN

BONNIE and ARTHUR GEISERT

HOUGHTON MIFFLIN COMPANY BOSTON 2000

Walter Lorraine Books

For Noah

Walter Lorraine Books

Library of Congress Cataloging-in-Publication Data
Geisert, Bonnie.
    Mountain town / Bonnie and Arthur Geisert.
        p.   cm.
    Summary: Describes a year in the present-day life of a mountain
town that was founded when prospectors searching for gold arrived in
the Rocky Mountains in the mid-nineteenth century.
    ISBN 0-395-95390-1
    [1. Mountain life — Fiction.   2. City and town life — Fiction.]
I. Geisert, Arthur.   II. Title.
PZ7.G2725Mo   2000
[E] — dc21   99-29856
                                                          CIP

Printed in the United States of America

WOZ   10   9   8   7   6   5   4   3   2   1

MOUNTAIN TOWN

During the last half of the nineteenth century, prospectors rushed to the Rocky Mountains, hoping to find gold and silver. Where the precious ores were found, towns sprang up within days. Eventually, the mines played out, people left, and towns disappeared. Most of the towns that survived were county seats, which served the needs of miners, ranchers, and other settlers who stayed.

In the past it was difficult to reach such a town, but today roads, bridges, and railways connect it to the world beyond.

It is early winter in the town, and already the mountains around it are covered with snow.

A large amount of snow falls in the mountains. It is possible to have snow any day of the year.

Often it snows throughout the night.

The people are used to living with the snow and continue
to go about their business.

But at times deep snow makes the mountain roads very dangerous.

The roads are plowed quickly after a storm so school and work can
continue with little interruption.

Fresh snow is a joy to skiers, and they stream into town, eager to try their skill on the snowy slopes.

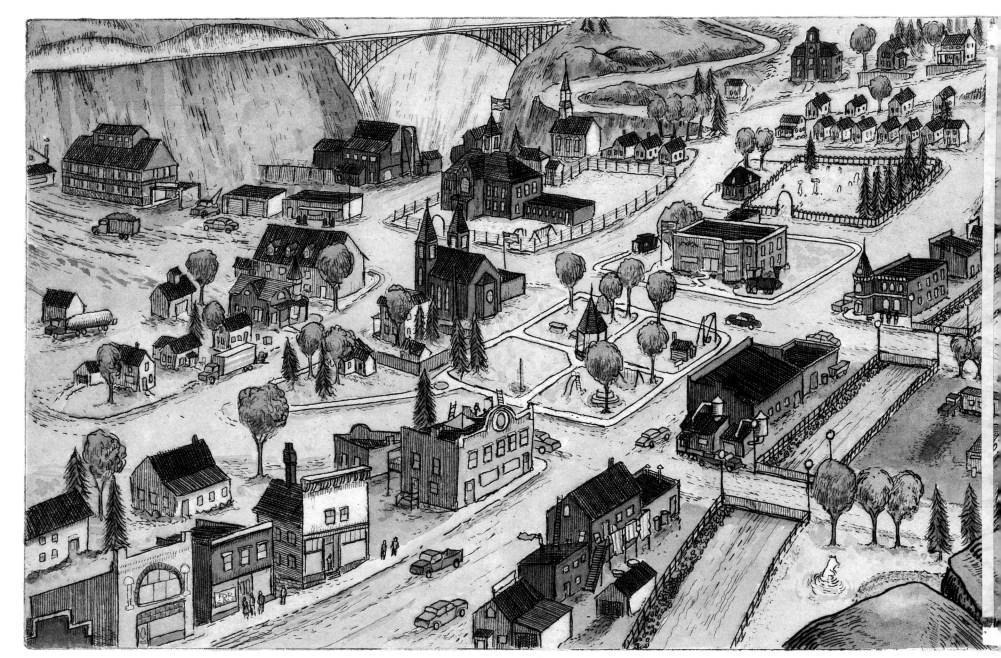

In the cool spring air, people hike the mountain trails, finding pleasure in the season's changes.

At a high spot, they stop to picnic and take pictures. The town provides a great backdrop for photographs.

The gold and silver mines that were once so important to the town
are now idle.

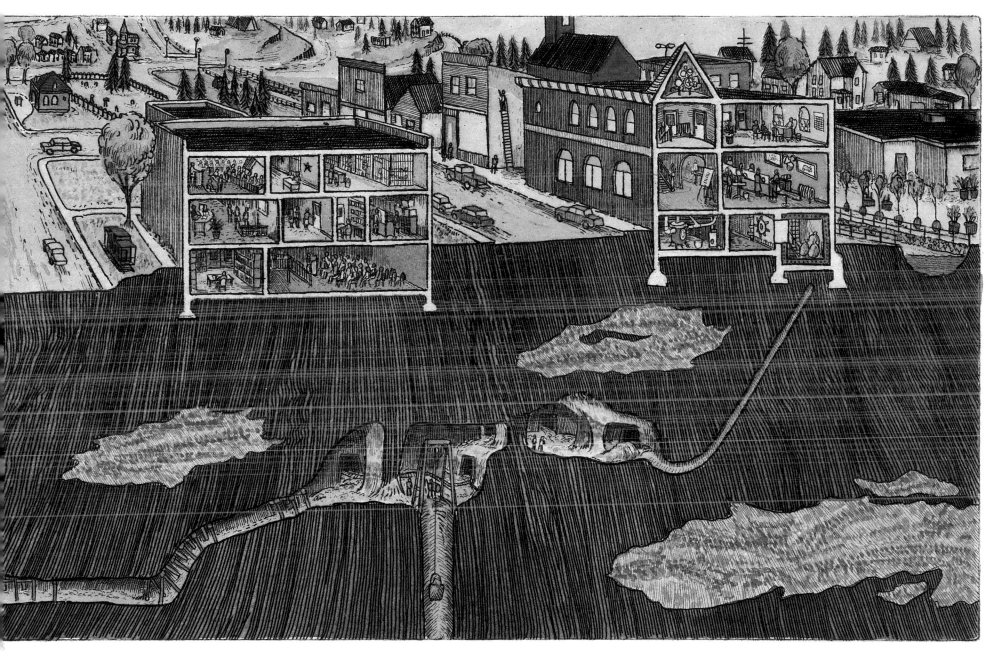

New companies now mine for other metals.

Some people take advantage of the tunnels to reach the bank vault.

But it is a long way from the vault to the mine opening, where
surprise waits for these self-proclaimed "miners."

Near a meadow where cows and calves graze, the road crew repairs the snowplows.

In town, people are happy that the drive-in café is open for the season.

On the Fourth of July, a big celebration takes place.

The town is packed with people.

Rafting down the swift mountain streams on inner tubes
is a summertime thrill.

During Heritage Days, old-timers enjoy the rock-drilling contests.

In late summer, thunderstorms roll over the mountains,
often with dangerous lightning.

This is a good time to take cover inside.

When school starts in the fall, the football team becomes
the center of attention.

The townsfolk crowd together to enjoy the game.

Before winter, the cattle are herded down from high pastures.

Salt is stockpiled at the county garage. Tons will be needed
to melt ice and snow on the steep, curvy roads.

When aspen leaves turn yellow, it will soon be winter.

The mountain town is ready for the season again.

A year has passed in the mountain town. The illustrations show stories of people's lives from day to day and season to season. The stories tell of work and play — and of wrongdoing.

There are some busy people and places in the town. One mine is very busy because trucks loaded with ore come and go often. The sawmill receives loads of logs to cut into lumber. Outside the grocery store, the produce changes with the seasons.

Three men with a dog and green pickup truck scheme to rob the mine and the bank. The bank later increases its security.

Some downtown apartment dwellers appear to practice the belief that "cleanliness is next to godliness." Residents move in and out of the mobile home section, taking their homes with them. A moving van reveals that a family is moving into a house, where eventually they build a dormer.

A chimney is destroyed by fire and rebuilt. An effigy of the school's mascot grizzly is built by play and destroyed by nature. The mascot makes special appearances on and off the football field.

The cemetery offers a clue that mourners had gathered at church for a funeral.

The only blue car in town seems to be everywhere. During winter, its owner has some unfortunate luck. That blue car is parked at home in the first and the last double-page illustrations.